The Obits

by

Dennis Doud

WordCrafts

The Obits
Copyright © 2015
Dennis Doud

All rights reserved. No part of this book may be reproduced, stored in a retrieval system, or transmitted in any form or by any means – electronic, mechanical, photocopy, recording, or otherwise – without the prior written permission of the publisher. The only exception is brief quotations for review purposes.

Published by **WordCrafts Theatrical Press**
Buffalo, Wyoming
www.wordcrafts.net

THE OBITS
Copyright © 2015, Dennis Doud

All Rights Reserved

CAUTION: Professionals and amateurs are hereby warned that performance of **The Obits** is subject to payment of a royalty. It is fully protected under the copyright laws of the United States of America, and of all countries covered by the International Copyright Union. All rights, including professional, amateur, motion picture, public reading, broadcast, and any other reproduction by means known or yet to be discovered are strictly reserved.

All rights are controlled exclusively by **WordCrafts Theatrical Press,** Buffalo, Wyoming. No performance of this play may be given without obtaining in advance the written permission of Wordcrafts Theatrical Press, and paying the requisite fee.

SPECIAL NOTE: Anyone receiving permission to produce **The Obits** is required to give credit to the Author as the sole and exclusive Author of the Play on the title page of all programs distributed in connection with performances of the Play and in all instances in which the title of the Play appears for purposes of advertising, publicizing or otherwise exploiting the Play. The name of the Author must appear on a separate line, in which no other name appears, immediately beneath the title and in size of type equal to 50% of the size of the largest, most prominent letter used for the title of the Play. No person, firm or entity may receive credit larger or more prominent than that accorded the Author.

The Obits

by

Dennis Doud

Characters
In Order of Appearance

Joseph "Joe" Guftason
Marlene Avery
Edgar "Eddie" Robinson
Woman from the County

SCENE I

SETTING: The café: 4 chairs, 2 tables set against a wall with a large picture window which allows customers to observe people as they walk by. A freshly folded newspaper sits on one table. A sign, downstage right, says "Day 1."

AT RISE: The door opens and closes, causing a tinny bell over the door to ring. **JOE**, a newly retired factory worker in his early 60s, enters. He is a first-time visitor to café. He always wears a beat up Dallas Cowboys hat. He looks around and sits down at the closest chair and table. He happily picks up the fresh newspaper on the table top and settles in. **MARLENE**, the matriarchal waitress, late 30s, hustles in from the kitchen (off-stage). She's nervous. Very nervous.

MARLENE
Hey, hun. Wouldn't you be more comfortable away from the window?

JOE
(**JOE** looks around and shakes his head.)
With my eyes, I need all the light I can get. Readin' gets tougher every year.

(**MARLENE** almost cringes when **JOE** pops the paper and folds it. She glances at her watch.)

MARLENE
Well, what can I getcha, hun? Sumthin' quick?

JOE
Just coffee. It's my first day of retirement and I wanna savor it.

(**MARLENE** exits and is instantly back with a cup of coffee. **MARLENE** steps to the window and looks down the street. **JOE** takes a sip and smiles.)

JOE
Good coffee and a fresh paper. Retirement's gettin' off on the right foot.

MARLENE
(Looks at her watch and mutters to herself.)
That won't last long.
(Starts to leave then stops to look out the window again. She turns to **JOE**.)
What's your name, hun?

JOE
Joe. Why?

MARLENE
Joe, I got a long-time, regular customer comin' in here real soon and with all he's been through, he's become kinduva creature ah habit.

JOE
Okay. So?

>(**JOE** looks at **MARLENE** who starts to fidget before coming clean.)

MARLENE
You're in his seat. And his table. And he'll be here in about a minute.

JOE
So...

MARLENE
If you'd just move over to this other table, the world's gonna be a whole lot nicer place to live in. And…

JOE
And, what?

MARLENE
And... Hey, the coffee's free! Whaddaya say? oh, crap...

>(**EDDIE** struggles into view outside the window. He sees **JOE** sitting in his chair and his eyes

go wide. He flails his hand and cane as unintelligible words are barely heard. **EDDIE** thumps past angrily. There's the door-and-bell sound and an agitated **EDDIE** wheezes int, cane thumping the floor. He stops near **JOE**.)

EDDIE
Whaddaya doin'?!

JOE
(Looks bewildered.)
What?

EDDIE
Whaddaya doin' in my seat?!

MARLENE
Now, Eddie, don't blow a fuse. The nice gentleman was just movin.' Right...nice gentleman?

(**Eddie** glares at **JOE**, who starts to lean forward with eyes narrowed. **JOE** takes a deep breath and gets ready to let **EDDIE** have it, when he sees **MARLENE** standing behind **EDDIE** with her hands clasped in prayer and pleading with her eyes. **JOE** releases the breath and bites his tongue.)

EDDIE
You...you get the...

JOE
Sorry, man. Didn't know it was yours.

MARLENE
Now, Eddie, just calm down.

JOE
I'll move.

> (**JOE** gets up and walks past a wheezing **EDDIE**, carrying his coffee and the paper. He sits down at another table and settles in. **EDDIE** plops into his chair, exhausted. He looks down at the table and starts getting worked up again. He points with his cane.)

EDDIE
Dang it, Marlene - he's got my paper!

> (**MARLENE** looks at **EDDIE** a long second. She steps between the two tables and looks at **JOE**. He looks over the paper at her. **MARLENE** turns so **EDDIE** can't see her and goes into the prayer grip and the pleading eyes as she nods her head toward **EDDIE**.)

MARLENE
Would ya give 'im the obits? Please?

JOE
The whats?

MARLENE
The obits. That's all he needs. The obits.

(**JOE** looks lost. **EDDIE** jumps in.)

EDDIE
The o-bit-u-air-ez!

(**JOE** scowls but catches Marlene's face. With a deep breath, he peels off the obits and, forcing a smile, hands them to **MARLENE,** who mouths "thank-you-thank-you" before she turns and drops them on Eddie's table. She turns to face downstage as she looks at the two men. She almost bows in Joe's direction as she nods his way.)

MARLENE
You, sir, are a gentleman.
(She waggles a finger first at JOE, then at **EDDIE.**)
And you, you cantankerous old fart, had better leave one heckuva tip when you're done or I'll have Bubba come out here. And you can't even outrun him

EDDIE
(Starts to say something but catches the look in Marlene's eye as she slowly points at him. He changes his mind.)
Yes, ma'am.

MARLENE

Good.

(**EDDIE** and **JOE** watch **MARLENE** exit. Both men go back to their paper and coffee. **EDDIE** nods and shakes his head as he makes small grunts, uh-uh, tongue clucks, and 'mmmm's' while reading. **JOE** looks over at him, watches briefly, then rolls his eyes. **JOE** puts the paper down by his cup and stands to leave. He mutters softly as he walks past **EDDIE**.)

JOE

Don't forget the tip or you'll be talkin' to Bubba.

EDDIE

(He doesn't look up from the obits.)

Shoot. Bubba's slower 'n me. Man's a glacier.

SCENE II

SETTING: The café: 4 chairs, 2 tables set against a wall with a large picture window which allows customers to observe people as they walk by. A freshly folded newspaper sits on one table. The sign, downstage right, says "Day 2."

AT RISE: **JOE**, limping slightly, walks past the backside of the window. There's the door-and-bell sound. **JOE** enters, walks to the first table, picks up the fresh paper, ruffles through it and peels off the obits. Leaving them by Eddie's chair, **JOE** walks to the other table and grimaces as he sits down. He rubs his knee briefly before settling back and popping open the paper. **MARLENE** comes over with a cup and a carafe.

    MARLENE
You are either the most pigheaded man I've met in sometime - or the dumbest.

    JOE
Yeah. I get that a lot.

MARLENE
(Cocks her head at him.)
Thanks for your help yesterday, hun.

JOE
No problem. Today I'm lookin' for a nice quiet cuppa coffee and the paper.

MARLENE
(Looks at her watch.)
Just remember ya said that. He ought to be here in two minutes. Less if he's got a tailwind.

JOE
He come in everyday?

MARLENE
Yeah. Ever since... yeah, every day.

(**MARLENE** exits. A moment later **EDDIE** wheezes up to the outside of the window. He sees **JOE**, stops, puts his head down, sighs heavily, then looks straight ahead. The door-and-bell sounds. **EDDIE** wearily enters and collapses in his chair. He straightens himself up and sits looking downstage. **JOE** looks over at him then goes back to reading. **EDDIE** glances at the table top and sees the obits, then looks back downstage. **MARLENE** enters and sets a cup down by the obits. **EDDIE** wheezes a smile.)

EDDIE
Thanks, Marlene.

MARLENE
Sure, hun.

(**MARLENE** exits. **EDDIE** picks up the obits and holds them slightly up while looking downstage.)

EDDIE
Thanks.

(**JOE** grunts and nods, not looking up from his paper. They read and sip. **EDDIE** starts his nodding and noises. **JOE** stops to refill his cup. He looks at **EDDIE**.)

JOE
You must know a lotta folks that died.

EDDIE
(Looks up from the obits, then over at **JOE**.)
Say what?

JOE
From the sound of it, you must know a lotta folks that have died.

EDDIE
Oh. No. No.
(Goes back to reading.)
Seems like some folks do a whole lot more

than others, accordin' to what's written.

JOE
(Shrugs, and goes back to his newspaper.)
I dunno 'bout that. The obituaries are like Christmas letters. Some are short and tell ya nuthin.' Others are long, brag a lot, and are full of enough B.S. to fertilize the back forty.

EDDIE
(Smiles in spite of himself. He lays the obits down with a nod.)
Yeah, I hear ya.

(**EDDIE** takes off his brand new Mavericks hat and runs a hand over his head. He then gently brushes at the Mavs hat with his fingertips before snugging it back in place. He picks up the obits and both men read for a little more. **EDDIE** drains his cup and puts it and the obits on the table. He stands up with effort, then looking downstage he touches the bill of his cap before exiting. **JOE** keeps looking at his paper but touches the bill on his Cowboys cap, too.)

SCENE III

SETTING: The café: 4 chairs, 2 tables set against a wall with a large picture window which allows customers to observe people as they walk by. A freshly folded newspaper sits on one table. The sign, downstage right, says "Day 3."

AT RISE: **JOE**, limping slightly, walks past the backside of the window and disappears off-stage. There's the door-and-bell sound. He stops at the first table, picks up the newspaper, shakes out the obits and takes the rest of the paper to his far chair. He sits down with a grunt, grimacing and rubbing his knee. Marlene enters with a cup and a carafe.

          MARLENE
What's with the knee, Joe?

          JOE
Ah, it's a history lesson that gives me a test now and then.

          MARLENE
I got some aspirin.

JOE
Nah. Thanks anyway. It just wakes up a bit later than the rest o' me. It'll come 'round.

> (**MARLENE** exits. **JOE** pops and folds the paper, pours a cup and begins to read. **EDDIE** appears moving slowly past the window, exits off-stage. The door-and-bell sounds, **EDDIE** slowly enters, sits down gingerly in "his" seat, sighing heavily. **MARLENE** enters with a cup. She puts it by the obits.)

EDDIE
Thanks, Marlene.

MARLENE
You bet, Eddie.
> (She exits.)

EDDIE
> (Takes a cautious sip before picking up the obits. He looks over at **JOE**, tipping the paper in Joe's direction.)

Thanks, man.

JOE
> (Nods, then puts his paper down, gets up and walks to **EDDIE**. He offers his hand.)

I'm Joe.

EDDIE
(Considers Joe's hand, then takes it as his defenses crumble.)
Nice to officially meet'cha, Joe. Name's Eddie. Well, to most folks it is. My mama called me 'Edgar' and my daddy called me 'Hey-YOU!'

JOE
(Smiles as he goes back to his chair and sits down.)
Yeah. I had an old-man like that, too. Swear every once in while I still hear 'im.

EDDIE
Ain't it the truth? I just remember that I never wanted to hear my mama use my middle name.

JOE
Yeah?

EDDIE
Meant the water was boilin' and I was in it deep.

(Both men chuckle. The quiet gets comfortable as they read.)

JOE
Here's an obit for ya. Swenson's is closin.'

EDDIE
Ahhh, man. The old Five & Dime? Shoot, that's a landmark. Been here since... uh...

JOE
Says here, 1969. Yeah. They opened my senior year of high school. The next year I was gonna go off to college. Instead I spent my freshman and sophomore years in 'Nam.

EDDIE
(Looks up and downstage, instantly going into a 1,000 yard stare, his voice getting softer.)
Lord knows that'll give ya an education.

JOE
Yeah. Yeah, it will. It's stuff that folks shouldn't hafta learn. The tests are - tough.
(**JOE** absently reaches for his knee and rubs it. Both men are staring downstage. **JOE** blinks and reaches for his cup.)
You ever in the service, Eddie?

EDDIE
No. No. They didn't want me. Tried. They took my boy, though.

JOE
(Starts to take a sip of coffee)
Oh?

EDDIE
Yeah. He went off to I-Rack. Never came back.

JOE
(His cup freezes in mid-air.)
Sorry, man.

EDDIE
Yeah. The tests are tough.
> (A small awkward silence, then **EDDIE** half-smiles and flutters the paper in his hand.)

That's when I started readin' the obits. Readin' what folks leave behind. What they'd done, who loved 'em, what folks remember 'bout 'em.
> (**JOE** nods. They turn back to their papers. **EDDIE** makes a few more nods-and-noises then sets the obits down. He struggles to his feet.)

You have a nice day, Joe.

JOE
You, too, Eddie. Sorry 'bout your boy. Take care.

> (They touch their hat brims in unison. **EDDIE** exits.)

SCENE IV

SETTING: The café: 4 chairs, 2 tables set against a wall with a large picture window which allows customers to observe people as they walk by. A freshly folded newspaper sits on one table. The sign, downstage right, says "Day 4."

AT RISE: **JOE** is seated at his table sipping coffee. **EDDIE** crosses past the outside the window before exiting upstage center right. **JOE** smiles at the door-and-bell sound and glances over. **EDDIE** enters and almost whispers the greeting.

   EDDIE
Mornin,' Joe.

   JOE
Mornin,' Eddie.

     (**EDDIE** plunks into his chair. **MARLENE** enters with his cup. She sets it down, looking concerned.)

   EDDIE
Thanks.

MARLENE
You OK, hun? Havin' one of those days?

EDDIE
Yeah. But... nuthin' coffee and... a... pretty smile can't fix.

MARLENE
I'll come back 'n' check on ya in awhile, OK, hun?

EDDIE
Thanks.

>(**MARLENE** exits. **EDDIE** and **JOE** sip and read. **EDDIE** stops his nods-and-noises to look at the ceiling downstage. He ponders something. A sad smile dawns on his face. He looks over at **JOE** and takes a deep breath, his voice coming out thin and strained.)

EDDIE
You married, Joe?

JOE
>(Glances over and sees **EDDIE** looking at him.)

I'm sorry, what?

EDDIE
>(Takes another deep breath and motions with his paper.)

You might as well sit over here. I ain't got the air to yell today.

(**JOE** pauses, then nods. He grimaces as he stands. He grabs his cup, carafe, and paper and sits down opposite **EDDIE** at his table. **EDDIE** takes a swig and a deep breath before continuing.)
What I said was, are you married, Joe?

JOE
Yeah. 39 years. You?

EDDIE
Was. She'd been fightin' cancer off 'n' on for, oh, 15 years. Found out she had it when the boy was about five. It'd go away, come back. Did that twice.

JOE
When did she pass?

EDDIE
(Squints downstage, looking past memories.)
It was 'bout a year after we got the news 'bout Johnnie. That... that took the fight right outta her.
(They both stare at their papers, neither one reading.)
Yeah. Today's our anniversary. Woulda been 42 years.

JOE
(Lowers his paper and nods.)
How long ya know each other before that?

EDDIE
(Breaks into a genuine grin.)

Joe, she was the first girl I ever walked home from school. The first girl I ever held hands with, hugged, or kissed. And on our weddin' night...
>(Both laugh and nod.)

She was a part o' me for a long, long time. The best part.
>(Drains his cup and sets it
>down with the obits.)

Good coffee.

JOE
It is, innit?

>(**MARLENE** enters carrying a refill pot. She walks to the table and stops.)

SCENE V

SETTING: The café: 4 chairs, 2 tables set against a wall with a large picture window which allows customers to observe people as they walk by. A freshly folded newspaper sits on one table.

AT RISE: A slow strobe flashes as the days pass. The sign randomly updates, revealing the passage of time. **EDDIE, JOE** and **MARLENE** enter and leave. the backdrop changes, the clothes change, but the ball caps always remain the same - a new "Mavericks" cap for **EDDIE** and a beat-up "Cowboys" cap for **JOE**. At the final strobe the sign says "Day 157," then the stage goes dark.

SCENE VI

SETTING: The café: 4 chairs, 2 tables set against a wall with a large picture window which allows customers to observe people as they walk by. The sign, downstage right, says "Day 158."

AT RISE: **JOE** is seated at Eddie's table, sipping coffee and reading. The obits are already neatly folded by Eddie's chair. There are two cups and a carafe on the table. The door-and-bell sounds. **EDDIE** struggles in. He groans as he sits down. JOE pours him a cup and slides it over to him.

       EDDIE
Thanks, Joe. Definitely need it today.

       JOE
Tough day?

       EDDIE
          (Taps his chest with agitation before taking a deep breath.)
The carburetors aren't workin' for diddly squat this mornin'. Makin' my motor work harder 'n usual.

                    JOE
                         (Lowers the paper to his lap.)
How long ya been like this?

                    EDDIE
Oh, seven, eight years. Gets kinda old.

                    JOE
So why walk? Ya got anyone to take ya around?

                    EDDIE
                         (Arches arches his back and
                         grimaces.)
County Services has a pickup and delivery
service, but shoot, Joe. Do I look like a
pizza to you?
                         (**JOE** laughs as **EDDIE** waves a
                         hand.)
Went in for my final appointment today. Doc
said keep walkin' if I can, if I want to. So,
I walk.
                         (**EDDIE** takes a swig and puts the
                         obits on his lap.)
Say, Joe. Anythin' in the paper 'bout the
Mavericks?

                    JOE
Mavericks. Let's see. Nope. I've noticed the
hat. You a fan?

                    EDDIE
                         (Pulls off the Mavs ball cap and
                         looks at it, brushing it off
                         gently, almost reverently, with
                         his fingers.)
Our boy, Johnnie, was five when the Mavs
started playin'. Yeah. He had dreams of

playin' for 'em. He practiced hard. Dribblin,' shootin.' Memorized names, stats.
> (Shakes his head and chuckles.)

But the boy was built like a fireplug. No, the Lord built 'im for the Marines, not the NBA.
> (Looks over and points with his chin.)

Whadda 'bout you and that raggedy Cowboys hat?

JOE
Bought this my senior year in high school. Had the same dream as Johnnie, 'cept I was gonna wear the Star and date one of those cheerleaders. I was 19 when I realized I wasn't big enough, and when I got back from 'Nam I only had one good knee.

> (Both men smile and turn back to their papers. Suddenly **EDDIE** looks downstage, a question forming on his face.)

EDDIE
Huh.

JOE
> (Looks over.)

What?

EDDIE
Ever wonder why dreams are never mentioned in the obits?

JOE
What's that?

EDDIE
The obits. They only tell ya what folks have done, not what they wanted to do; what they dreamed they'd be.
>   (**JOE** grunts and nods.)
Just seems that the obits oughta paint a bigger picture, so folks would kinda know the person.

>   (They both look downstage over their papers, both seeing the same thing.)

JOE
Like a person's life should be more'n just a few sentences.

EDDIE
Yeah. Even if they weren't famous they were still - sumbody.
>   (His face contorts as he tries to corral a thought, then he catches it.)
There was this poem I heard in school. Nobody's an island. And we're all connected, somehow. Yeah. Guess there's dreams in every one ah us.

JOE
Hmm. Pretty deep thinkin,' Eddie.

EDDIE
Gotta be this coffee, Joe.
>   (Puts the cup and the obits on the table and fights to his feet.)
You take care now.

                    JOE
You, too, man.

                         (They touch their brims in
                         unison.)

SCENE VII

SETTING: The café: 4 chairs, 2 tables set against a wall with a large picture window which allows customers to observe people as they walk by. The sign, downstage right, says "Day 159."

AT RISE: **JOE** is seated at Eddie's table, sipping coffee and reading. The obits are folded neatly next to a cup by Eddie's chair. A minute passes. **JOE** leans back to look out the window. He goes back to reading. He turns a page, then looks at his watch as he furrows his brow. He finishes the page, sets the paper down, and drains his cup. He stands and walks out of the café causing the door chime to ring.

SCENE VIII

SETTING: The café: 4 chairs, 2 tables set against a wall with a large picture window which allows customers to observe people as they walk by. The sign, downstage right, says "Day 160."

AT RISE: **JOE** is seated at Eddie's table, sipping coffee and reading. The obits are folded neatly next to a cup by Eddie's chair. The **WOMAN FROM THE COUNTY** passes outside the window. The door-and-bell sounds and **JOE** looks expectantly at the door. He is disappointed to see the **WOMAN** enter. He goes back to his paper. The **WOMAN** crosses to the table and stops beside **JOE**. She is holding a large, clasped manila envelope.

      WOMAN
Are you Joe?

      JOE
Yes, ma'am.

      WOMAN
I'm with County Services. And, um, Edgar

Robinson passed away yesterday. He left you this.
> (She holds out the envelope. **JOE** drops his paper on the table, hesitating before taking the envelope.)

He said that you would know what to do with it.
> (**JOE** stares at the envelope, puzzled.)

Joe? Are you okay?

JOE
What? Oh. Yeah. Thanks. Thank you.
> (**WOMAN** starts to leave.)

Ma'am, uh, didn't he have any family?

WOMAN
No, I'm afraid not. He was predeceased by his parents, brothers, wife, and son.

> (**JOE** sits staring at the envelope. The **WOMAN** waits for a moment, then discreetly exits, causing the the door-and-bell to sound, startling **JOE**. He looks up and around, then back at the envelope. He gently opens it and pulls out some stapled pages. He smiles as he reads the first page.)

JOE
The Obit of Edgar Glenford Robinson.
> (Shakes his head and chuckles.)

Heckuva middle name, Eddie.

>   (Settles back and reads. His
>   eyes don't leave the page as he
>   reaches for his coffee. He nods
>   and smiles.)

So, you wanted to be a superhero.
>   (Takes a swig.)

And a fireman.
>   (Reads a bit more.)

And own a brand new Camaro.
>   (Sets his cup down, picks up the
>   envelope, reaches in and pulls
>   out the Mavericks ball cap. He
>   pops it out to normal shape and
>   holds it up. He gently brushes
>   it off with his fingertips. He
>   reaches across the table to put
>   the cap on the obits. He pours
>   Eddie's cup full of coffee, and
>   touches the brim of his ball cap
>   before taking a swig himself.
>   Looking at the obit, he sits back
>   into his chair. The stage lights
>   start a slow fade as he continues
>   reading. He sets the obit down
>   on the table, sits up straight
>   and looks over at Eddie's chair,
>   waving the cup in that
>   direction.)

Really? A duet with Sinatra?

Curtain

ABOUT THE AUTHOR

Dennis Doud was born in the same hospital as John Wayne, and lived his entire childhood in Iowa before leaving for higher education. After graduating from LeTourneau College, (now a university), in Longview, Texas, he returned home to the Hawkeye State.

He left Iowa again to chase down his almost-a-wife who had taken a job in the Northwoods of Wisconsin. It's a place called "God's Country" and it has been truly that to Dennis, his bride of 35 years, and their now-grown-up kids.

Dennis has enjoyed reading and writing since elementary school, but to this day he still barely tolerates arithmetic. He has written numerous short stories and articles, and has now trying his hand at writing faith-based screenplays and 'tweener home-school adventure books. He sporadically scribbles an online blog called *Uncle Denny's Garage*. Follow him online at:

www.headwaterswordsmithing.com

Also Available From

WordCrafts Theatrical Press

Jane Austen's Pride & Prejudice
  by Paula K. Parker

Oscar Wilde's Dorian Gray
  by Mike Parker

Charles Dickens' A Christmas Carol
  by Ronnie Meek

www.wordcrafts.net

www.ingramcontent.com/pod-product-compliance
Lightning Source LLC
Chambersburg PA
CBHW072115290426
44110CB00014B/1928